More Worship With Kids!

Planting Seeds

Kate Finney

More Worship With Kids!
Planting Seeds
by Kate Finney

© 2017 Kate Finney All Rights Reserved.

No part of this book may be reproduced in any manner whatsoever without prior written permission from the publisher and author. The exception would be in the case of brief quotations embodied in critical articles and reviews and pages where permission is specifically granted by the publisher or author.

Although every precaution has been taken to verify the accuracy of information contained herein, the author and publisher assume no responsibility for any errors or omissions. No liability is assumed for damages that may result from the use of information contained within.

Scripture quotations taken from The Holy Bible, New International Version® NIV®.
Copyright © 1973, 1978, 1984, 2011 by Biblica, Inc. ™
Used by permission. All rights reserved worldwide.

Produced by Kate Finney, Worship With Kids!
Cover Photo: Samantha Pentelow and Carleah Morrison

Printed by CreateSpace, An amazon.com Company.
Available from amazon.com and other book stores.

Library of Congress Catalog Number: 9780998237626

ISBN: 978-0-9982376-2-6
ISBN-13: 0998237620

First Edition. Printed in the United States

Religion/Christian Education/Children & Youth | Christian Ministry/Children | Education

DEDICATION

To my parents, Karen, George, Ron & Harriet,
who taught me *how* to plant seeds

He told them another parable: "The kingdom of heaven is like a mustard seed, which a man took and planted in his field. Though it is the smallest of all seeds, yet when it grows, it is the largest of garden plants and becomes a tree, so that the birds come and perch in its branches."
Matthew 13:31-32

CONTENTS

STORY	LESSON | BIBLE VERSE	Page
Planting Seeds in Winter	Plant seeds of God's love in any season Mark 8:1-20	1
What Do Butterflies Do on a Windy Day?	Nature teaches us perseverance	3
My Compass	Jesus shows us the right direction Hebrews 13:7-16 & Matthew 28:19-20	5
New Path	Trust God during times of change Proverbs 2:9-22	7
We Are the Metal; He Is the Magnet	Nothing can separate us from God's love Romans 8:31-39	9
Never Too Many Black Raspberries	Share what you do not need Matthew 13:1-12	11
Dirty Window	Rely on God's perspective, not yours Proverbs 3:5-6	13
Being Brave	Trust God and He will make you brave Refers to David, Noah, Daniel, Peter & James	15
Scary Neighbors	Everyone is my neighbor Luke 10:29-37	17
Five Ways for Shy People to Evangelize	You don't have to be outgoing to evangelize	19
Using an Interpreter	Ask for help from church members	21
What Makes You Kind	Our behavior shapes who we are Matthew 5:38-42	23
What's the Word?	Exploring different versions of the Bible	25
A Distinctive Walk	Defining the character of a faith walk 2 Timothy 1:7	27
Looking Through the Screen	Seeing others and ourselves from the inside first	29
Pulling Dandelions	Follow the Golden Rule Matthew 7:12	31
...that's What Little Bells Are Made of	Shape your life with God's teachings	33

STORY	LESSON | BIBLE VERSE	Page
How You Cut the Deck	The Good News changes the Bible Malachi 4:5-6	37
Twist Ties Don't Last Forever	Life is short - Serve today Matthew 25:23 & Peter 4:10-11	39
Holy Jeans	Treat yourself like a child of God Genesis 1:26 & Gal 3:23-29	41
True Reflections	Searching for and being positive influences	43
Bread or Cookies - Yes!	God doesn't play favorites Matthew 7:9-11	45
Joseph Glows In the Dark (Good Friday/Lent)	Joseph of Arimathea story Luke 23:44-56	47
We Are Waiting (Advent)	Being hope Titus 2:11-13	49
No Need to Wait - Love is Here! (Advent)	Christ's love lives in us 1 Cor 13:4-7 & Matthew 25:44-46	51
Joy of the Wise Men (Advent)	Joy is more than just great happiness Matthew 2:9-10	53
Peace Like a River (Advent)	Rivers are examples of true peace John 7:37-38	55

ACKNOWLEDGMENTS

I am grateful for all of the people who have contributed to this project. Most especially, I would like to thank Paul Nye, Linda Starr, Marilla Shafer, Carleah Morrison, Xavier Russell and Matthew Finney for their assistance in developing ideas and trying out these stories with me.

I would also like to thank all of the children at the Plymouth Church of the Brethren and its congregation, who teach me so much and allow me to teach them - through stories.

A special thank you goes to White River Zip Lines, in Indianapolis, IN for the great introduction to zip-lining.

PLANTING SEEDS IN WINTER

Get Yourself Focused

Plants and seeds are used throughout the Bible to talk about God's message of love to us as his children. This is a new twist on that familiar theme, reminding the kids that any season is a good season to start spreading God's word.

Preparation

- Read Mark 4:1-20

- Bring spring and winter garden pictures

- Bring packets of seeds to pass out to the kids at the end of the story

The Story

I brought some pictures to share with you today. This was my garden last spring. Look at all of those flowers and how green the leaves are. It looks wonderful, doesn't it? These flowers right here, the purple ones, smell heavenly. I'll have to bring some to show you next spring. Here is what the same section of my garden looks like this morning. Not the same at all, is it?

In nature, winter is a time of rest. Flowers and tress sleep - sometimes we call it going "dormant". They don't use as much energy and they don't need as much sun and water, because they aren't growing and blooming above the ground. They are waiting for better weather and conserving their strength for the growing season.

I love gardening. Even in winter, I am making plans for all of the things I want to do as soon as it gets warm. I order plants and seeds to arrive in time for spring. I draw pictures of where I want to put new plants in my garden [*Bring an example, if you have one.*]

making sure I consider the plants that are already there. I don't go out and weed or water my plants or pick vegetables. Those are all gardening activities for other seasons. You know what I do in every season, though? I plant seeds.

Did you know that in the Bible, the word of God is called a "seed"? What do you think that might mean? In Mark, Chapter 4, Jesus tells a parable about a farmer who goes out sowing seeds on his land. One gets eaten by birds; one falls on a ground that is too rocky to grow in; another falls among thorns and gets choked by all of the weeds around it. Then, there is one that falls on good soil and grows and grows, until it is a crop 100 times bigger than the seed that was sown!

God calls us to spread His word, everywhere we go. Just like planting seeds in our yards. As the seeds begin to grow in other persons' hearts, then they hear the call too and the word of God spreads to be much bigger than the original seed. We don't have to wait until Spring to begin sowing those kinds of seeds. The sooner we get started, the more time the seed will have to grow.

I have a packet of seeds for each of you to take home with you today. Hopefully, you will be able to plant some of them this week and be able to start watching them grow. While you watch them, think about ways that you can share God's message that He loves everyone, with friends and family.

Let us pray...

God, we are beginning to know what the Bible says and about all of the gifts and promises You have given us. We want to share what we know with others. Be with us as we plant your seeds of love with people we see each day. In your precious name we pray, Amen.

WHAT DO BUTTERFLIES DO ON A WINDY DAY?

Get Yourself Focused

The Bible isn't the only place to go for good lessons. Nature is sometimes the best teacher. By observing the world around us, we can learn all sorts of valuable things, like the importance of perseverance that I learned from the butterfly in this story.

Preparation

- Bring a picture of a butterfly

The Story

I was taking a walk the other day and it was windy! My hair was blowing in my face and the flags in the park were wrapped around their poles. I watched some leaves blow by, too quick to catch and then…I saw a butterfly. And I thought to myself - "What do butterflies do on a windy day?" I watched it for a while to see if it would tell me the answer. Here is what I found out:

- They flap their wings harder
- They change direction
- They don't stop flying

The butterfly taught me some good lessons, so I thought I should share them with you. When life seems really "windy" and things are difficult, what to do you do? Sometimes, it's easiest to just quit and say "Well, I guess I can't do it." or "That's OK, I didn't really want to do that anyway." There are some things in life that just weren't meant to be and it's OK to quit when something doesn't seem right for us, but when we try something new and we are sure we want to do it, we should behave like a butterfly.

- They flap their wings harder. That butterfly in the park did not stop flapping his wings once, as he was trying to push against the wind. He had someplace to be and he was determined to get there.
- They change direction. When the butterfly couldn't make any headway by just flapping harder, he changed the direction he was going and tried to fly into the wind at an angle, so he didn't have to fly so hard. If something isn't working, it doesn't always mean we need to quit. It may just mean we need to try to do it differently.
- They don't stop flying. I watched the butterfly for almost 20 minutes and no matter what happened to him, he did not stop. He had to try all sorts of different things and he must have been getting tired, but he kept going. Slowly, he made his way across the park. Things may take longer than we expect, but we will get there eventually, if we don't stop trying.

I don't know if butterflies pray, but we do. The greatest thing about having a little trouble in our lives is that we don't have to go through it alone. God will always help us, when we ask.

Let's ask him right now.

Let Us Pray

Heavenly Father, each of us has difficulties we face in our lives and you know what they are. Bless us as we face a new week and strive to be who you made us to be. Help us to know you are with us and encourage us to keep going, no matter what we are doing. In your name we pray, Amen.

MY COMPASS

Get Yourself Focused

Our world seems to have more distractions in it every day. At times, it may seem like we can't decide which direction to go or what to do next. That's what makes Jesus' steadfast love so great. It is constant, never changing and it can always point us in the right direction.

Preparation

- Read Hebrews 13:7-16 and Matthew 28:19-20

- Bring a compass. To make the story more interesting for the kids, have one or two of them hold the compass, when you do the experiment about changing direction.

The Story

I brought a compass with me today. You all know what a compass does, right? It points North. What else does it do? Anything? How about this question - What makes it point South? How about Southwest, isn't that where tornados come from?

Well, let's try a little experiment and maybe we can figure out what else a compass does. I happen to know that this way [*Point North in the sanctuary*] is North, so the needle on our compass is pointing there now. I'm going to spin around real fast and face South and see if my compass points South. Hmm. The needle moved, didn't it? It swung around when I turned the compass, but then it swung right back to North. Let me just turn a little this time. If that [*Point North*] is North and that [*Point South*] is South, then this [*Point West*] must be West and that makes right about here, Southwest [*Turn to face Southwest*]. It adjusted itself again to point North.

So, a compass points North really well. Based on that fact, we can tell where we are and what direction we are going. We can always correct our direction by looking at the compass and seeing where it is pointing. That's really amazing.

Now do you know the second thing a compass does? It does not change. It does one thing and it does it really well, no matter what. That reminds me of a Bible verse. In Hebrews 13:8, it says "Jesus Christ is the same yesterday and today and forever." Jesus is someone who is easy to follow! He is always pointing the same direction. So, when we get off track, we can just look to Him and adjust our course. If it doesn't look like we are going North, we can change to match Him.

Even if we spin around in circles a bunch, when we stop and look at His needle, it will still point the way we should go. There isn't a place you can go or a time in past, present or future where Jesus won't be with you to guide you. Matthew 28:20b says "And surely I will be with you always to the very end of the age."

Let us pray…

Jesus we count on you to help us know which way to go. Thank you for being unchanging and steadfast in your love and guidance. In your name we pray. Amen.

NEW PATH

Get Yourself Focused

God sees the big picture. A lot of times, when a change seems like a sad event it turns out to be happy, because God knew we needed to change direction to get on the right path.

Preparation

- Read Proverbs 2:9-22 and Proverbs 3:5

Story

My family and I spend a lot of time walking in our woods. I walk there to exercise and pray. My son plays with his friends, having adventures and building forts. The dog loves to go on hikes with us, exploring all of the good smells and sounds that are much more interesting than his yard.

A couple of years ago, a big storm came through our woods and knocked down many of our trees. Some of them were tall and wide and when they fell, they hit other trees and knocked them over too. Some of the trees were torn out of the ground by the roots.

After the storm, it was difficult to walk in our woods. It made me sad to see all of the crushed plants and fallen trees, many still with hundreds of green leaves on them. The forester said we needed to leave the trees for a while before we cut them up, so they would be hollow and easier to move. It was frustrating to find a way to walk in the woods. It seemed each time I would try to take a path, I would run into a tree blocking the way or so many limbs that I couldn't find where the path had been. I felt like a fine, peaceful place had been taken from me.

The Bible reminds us that when destruction and chaos happens in our lives, God does not leave us there. He leads us to better places. Many of the places we end up after upset in our lives, were not places you could get to using the paths we had been on.

Yesterday, our family took a walk in the woods and I realized something. We have made new paths, in order to avoid the fallen trees and the holes they left. I see familiar places from a different angle and walk in places I had not before. There are new trees too. We were finally able to clear away most of the fallen trees and the ones that remain are homes for animals and new places for my son to play. The woods are more beautiful than before, and just as peaceful.

Let Us Pray…

Lord, when we are in the midst of change, help us to focus on Your loving care and to trust that Your plan has a good place for us in it. Amen.

WE ARE THE METAL, HE IS THE MAGNET

Get Yourself Focused

Romans 8 has always been one of my favorite passages in the Bible. When sad, difficult and even tragic things happen, we can turn to this chapter to remind ourselves that our relationship with God is solid, no matter what is happening in the world.

Preparation

- Read Romans 8:31-39

- Bring a couple of pieces of metal and a magnet

Story

I was rearranging our refrigerator door the other day (we keep all sorts of reminders and pictures on it) and I couldn't get one of the magnets to come off. It was really strong! I had to slide it off the edge of the door and let it fall into my hand to get it to unstick. It reminded me of our relationship with God. Strong and impossible to separate.

Magnets are fascinating. I brought one with me today. They stick to most kinds of metal and you don't have to use glue or anything to make them stick there. See, if I get the magnet just close to the metal, it jumps right to it and sticks - all by itself. The metal can't stick to anything by itself, but the magnet can pull the metal to it.

Have you ever taken a piece of metal and magnetized it? You brush the magnet across the metal several times, until it has some of the magnetic charge. Then the metal can attract other pieces of metal and make them stick. [Demonstrate all of this, as you talk] It wears off after a while, though, and you have to re-magnetize the metal.

All of this is just like God and us. We are the metal, God is the magnet. He pulls us to Him and doesn't let go. We can be magnetized to do great things, but we have to stay in close touch with Him to keep it going. We don't have any power on our own. No matter what we do. God's love will not leave us.

Sometimes, we put things between us, like too many pieces of paper and the magnet falls off the fridge. But the papers fall off too and all we have to do is stick the magnet back on, with just the papers God wants to help us hold in place - just enough activities and events in our lives that are good for us.

One of my favorite passages in the Bible is Romans 8:35-39 [*Read the passage*]. Many times in my life when things have been going wrong or bad things are happening. I turn to those verses and they put everything into perspective. There is nothing…absolutely nothing, that can separate us from God and His love.

Let Us Pray…

Lord, thank you for Your Love. So strong and powerful that it surrounds us and holds us close to you, no matter what we or anyone else does. We are grateful that we cannot be separated from You - by anything. In your name we pray, Amen.

NEVER *TOO MANY* BLACK RASPBERRIES

Get Yourself Focused

This lesson is one that would be good to use in combination with a service project at your church. Organizations like Heifer International embrace this idea and put it into practice every day. It is not bad to wish for more than you need. The important thing is what you do with it, when you get it.

Preparation

- Read Matthew 13:1-12

Story

At our house, when the black raspberries begin to come on, there are tons of blossoms, which is pretty to look at, but it is also an indication of how many berries we will have in a few weeks. The more blossoms there are, the more berries we are going to have.

My family loves black raspberries. We put them on ice cream, make jam with them, have them for an afternoon snack with a glass of milk. My son's favorite way to eat them is while he is picking them. He never comes back from picking raspberries with more than 4 or 5 in his container. He picks a lot, but somehow they never quite make it to the house! Do you have a favorite thing you like to eat - maybe something that you can't wait to eat and then eat too much when you get the chance?

Well, our family is definitely blessed with too many black raspberries. Even when we pick quarts and quarts for several weeks, we can't get them all. They grow around the edge of our yard and back into our woods. Some of them are behind other plants with thorns or across the swampy ravine that is too mushy to walk in. Others are on bushes that have grown so tall we can't reach them, without a ladder. Some people might say we have too many black black raspberries. But, I don't think so, because you know what? Whenever I have more than I need, I share.

In Matthew 13:12 it says "For to him who has will more be given, and he will have abundance; but from him who has not, even what he has will be taken away." Jesus said this following a story about several servants who were each given money by their master and he rewarded the one who invested it and made it grow, but he took everything away from the man who hid it and just tried to keep it. We should never be greedy and want to have everything our own way or to keep it for ourselves or just the people we love best. We should want more than we need, so we can share with others and make God's generous gifts grow. It is important to want others to have blessings too, sometimes more than us. It is part of loving our neighbor as ourselves.

Let Us Pray…

Lord, thank you for all of the blessings you give us. Guide us in our attitudes toward what we have and help us to know what to do with the "extra" blessings you give us. In your heavenly name we pray, Amen.

DIRTY WINDOW

Get Focused

Sometimes our point of view gets clouded or dirty. We don't realize it, so we continue to use what we see to make judgments and take action. When we continually come back to God for guidance and advice, he cleans up our view and lets us make better decisions.

Preparation

- Adapt this story to a window you have or share it as a story about someone you know

- Read Proverbs 3:5-6

The Story

I was looking out my office window the other day. It was a beautiful, sunny day and the sunlight was streaming in the windows lighting up the whole room, every single corner. You know what kind of day I mean?

As I was looking at the edge of our yard, right near the woods, I saw something that looked like a small animal. I stopped what I was doing and studied it, trying to figure out what it was. It was bigger than a squirrel, but it wasn't quite big enough to be a groundhog. It was lighter in color, there were no stripes anywhere, so it couldn't be a raccoon or a skunk. "Maybe it was one of the neighbors' dogs or a cat?" I thought.

It didn't move for a really long time and neither did I. Finally, I got curious what this mysterious animal was and I got up and went out on my front porch to get a better look at it. When I got to the porch, though, it was gone. I couldn't see anything like it anywhere. "I must have scared it away." I thought. Too bad, because I really wanted to know what it was.

I went back into my office and sat down. I turned to look out the window and there it was, again - in the same spot. I couldn't believe it. How was that possible? I got up and walked closer to the window and all of a sudden, I realized what it was. It was a big blob of something that had gotten smudged on the outside of my window! It wasn't an animal at all. It was dirt.

Sometimes, our view of our own lives is like my dirty window. We look at things the way the world wants us to. We worry about money or success or beating someone else, instead of taking care of our neighbor and asking God what he wants us to do. The view the world is giving us, isn't real. It's nothing more than mud slung on the window during a rainstorm.

[Read Proverbs 3:5-6] God doesn't want us to rely on our own understanding of the world. Or anyone else's. He wants us to rely solely on Him. When we do that, we won't waste time on things that don't matter and we won't ever look silly.

Let us pray...

Dear God, we need you to guide us every day, even in the small things. Help us not to get confused by what we see and hear. In your name we pray, Amen.

BEING BRAVE

Get Yourself Focused

Being brave is not the same as being fearless. Everyone is afraid of something. Bravery is doing something, while you are still afraid. Put your trust in God and you can do things that scare you.

Preparation

- You can choose a time in your life when you were scared to do something, but did it anyway. Zip-lining is my story, but you can make it your own.

Story

Have any of you ever been zip-lining? Did you like it? A few months ago, I decided to go zip-lining, to face my fear of heights and conquer it…instead, I got a big surprise. Let me tell you about it.

I signed up to go with a couple of friends to do a 10-line course. Each line was a little bit harder than the one before and there were 3 bridges that dangled over the trees that we had to cross to get to some of the lines. I prayed to God and asked him to help me not be scared. I told Him that I trusted everything was in His hands and that I knew He would take care of me.

It was 60 degrees and raining that day. Those were miserable conditions to go zip-lining! As the day went on, it rained harder and harder making the lines wet and faster than usual. The wood tree stands, where we stopped in between the lines, were wet and slippery and the breeze blew the stands back and forth a little, as we stood on them.

Every time I jumped off the stand and zipped down a line, I trusted God would take care of me, but I was still terrified. I didn't understand why. I thought by the end of the day, I wouldn't be afraid of heights anymore. That evening, as I was thinking about my day, I remembered what a wise person told me once, "Bravery is not being fearless. Bravery is doing something while you are still afraid."

There are lots of stories of people being brave in the Bible. David killed a giant; Noah and his family survived a storm in an ark with a bunch of animals; Peter and James left their jobs as fishermen and followed Jesus when they had only just met Him; Daniel went into the lion's den and came out unharmed. They were all ordinary people like you and me. They just decided to trust that God would take care of them and took a leap of faith.

I went zip-lining to conquer my fear of heights. What I learned is that I can't. I will always be scared of heights, but I can go zip-lining and do all sorts of other things that terrify me, because I trust God. My big surprise is that I am brave! You are brave too. All you need to do is trust God and you will be able to do things that scare you.

Let Us Pray…

God, thank you for making us brave, even when we are unsure or afraid. Help us to trust you in everything we do and to look to you for guidance in all things. In your name we pray. Amen.

SCARY NEIGHBORS

Get Yourself Focused

The news media, politicians and advertisers talk about people in terms of demographics and statistics. Our world is full of ways to separate and define 'types' of people. Jesus makes it clear that the term "neighbor" transcends all labels and includes people not in the same *category* as we are. When the Bible says "Love your neighbor as yourself", it means we must love ALL people as ourselves. Even if they are very different from us.

Preparation

- Read Luke 10:29-37

The Story

When I was a kid, we lived in a neighborhood with a cul-de-sac, you know, you drive in at one end and at the other end, you go around a circle and drive back out. Well on that circle, we had several neighbors that our family was close to. Every year on the 'minor' holidays, like Labor Day, New Year's Day and Memorial Day, all of us would get together and have brunch at someone's house. We pitched in good food and the kids would play games or run around outside. The grown ups lingered over coffee and talk about their families and careers. We had a great time. That's what I usually think of when I think of neighbors.

One year at Halloween, my sister and I were on our way back home from trick-or-treating in the neighborhood. There were kids everywhere going door to door and parents standing on the street talking. We walked around the corner of one of the houses and a man jumped out of the bushes in a crazy costume! He said "Trick or Treat little kiddies!" in a high-pitched voice and jumped up and down like a madman. My little sister screamed and I just stood there paralyzed, not knowing what to do. Inside my heart was beating really fast and I was scared! Who was this man!? His hair was sticking out all over the place, his clothes looked dirty and torn. He had crooked teeth and some of them were missing, and his eyes… wait a minute. I looked at his eyes. I knew those eyes. I knew this man. It was our neighbor from across the street. He was a nice man, who was good friends with my dad. There was no reason to be scared. He was just being silly for Halloween. He pulled a couple of candy bars out of his pocket and put them in our bags. Then my sister realized who he was too. "Happy Halloween" he cackled and danced away.

Who is our neighbor? How will you know if you run in to him on the street? Will you recognize him if he doesn't look like you expect him too? Will he scare you, if he or she isn't like most of the people you already know? In Luke 10:29-37, Jesus answers the question "who is my neighbor" by telling the good Samaritan story. [*Read the passage, if time. Summarize briefly, if not.*]

Lots of times, our neighbor does not look like us or act like us. Sometimes, our neighbor is not right near us, they are someone who lives across town or across the ocean. Jesus' story tells us that all other people are our neighbors and we should love them as ourselves.

Let us pray…

Lord, when we meet our neighbor, whether they are like us or not, allow us to see them as important and special. Show us what they need and how we can treat them as we wish to be treated. In your name we pray. Amen.

FIVE WAYS FOR SHY PEOPLE TO EVANGELIZE

Get Yourself Focused

Not everyone is outgoing and comfortable talking with others about their Christian experience. Some people are not comfortable talking with others at all. Just because you are shy does not mean you can't evangelize, though. Here are some ideas of how to do it - your way.

Preparation

- You don't need anything, but yourself

Story

When I was a kid, it used to make me so nervous when we talked about Evangelism at church. Often, a really outgoing person would tell us a story about how they had shared the Good News of Jesus with a total stranger. Then they would say everyone should want to do it, because it was what being a good Christian was all about.

I was shy and really quiet when I was younger. I was sometimes uncomfortable talking to people I knew about personal subjects, let alone a stranger. Now that I'm older, I understand what evangelism is all about, though, and it isn't just being outgoing and *telling* everyone about Jesus. There are lots of different ways to share the Love of Christ with other people. Each person needs to find the way they want to do it and there is no one right way.

Here are 5 ideas for how to share Christian Love with other people, even if you are shy:

Be a helper. Help others do things, like mow the lawn, carry stuff, clean their house, practice a sport, do homework. You don't have to say a word. Just do - with them. All of the disciples in the Bible were helpers to others.

Be an example. Behave the way Jesus did when He was with people. He was kind, generous, loving, forgiving, put others first. Eventually, others will see what you are doing and want to be like you. That will give you the opportunity to show them how to follow Jesus.

Be present. When you are with other people, you don't have to say a lot or make yourself noticed. Just being present with other people makes them feel familiar and comfortable with you. They will get to know you and trust you. Just be with others as quietly as you like.

Be brave. Sometimes, being with people you don't know well may seem scary. Be with people anyway. The more you do something that scares you, the less it bothers you. God will be with you. Learn to feel His presence and you will be less afraid. He will guide you.

Be you. People hear God in lots of different ways. We are all made in His image, so part of God must be shy too. Do what you are comfortable doing and God will put a person who needs to hear His message in front of you. Maybe it will be someone shy - like you.

Let Us Pray…

Lord thank you for making some of us shy. Your message does not have to be shouted from a stage to be true. We can whisper it and model it to our friends and neighbors and it will be heard just as clearly. Speak through us. Amen.

USING AN INTERPRETER

Get Focused

The lessons in the Bible don't always make sense without guidance from other Christians who are more experienced than we are. We can rely on the wisdom of other people in our church to help us interpret what we read.

Preparation

- Read John 1:1-5

The Story

Bon Jour! Comment allez-vous! How many of you understood what I just said? If you didn't understand what I said in French, what did that feel like? I said "Good morning, how are you?" Sometimes it is difficult to understand things when you don't have someone to interpret them for you.

I learned French in high school and one summer in college, I went on a study abroad trip and had the chance to test my skills in real life. The very first thing I needed to do when I got to Paris was take the Metro (that's what they call their underground subway) to the center of of the city. I stood in a long line and when I got to the window, I gave my money and asked for some tokens. The attendant answered me in French, but I didn't quite understand him, so I asked him to repeat what he had said. He said it again and I thought I understood the words, but it didn't make any sense to me. I thought he said "I won't give you a token, because you have to change." So, I asked him "Change what?". He repeated what he had said again and this time, he was irritated.

I looked at my money. I knew I had more than enough to pay for the tokens, but I couldn't figure out what I needed to change. So, I asked him if I could just have one token. Then he got really mad and shouted "No, change, change!".

All of a sudden, I realized what he was saying. He didn't want me to "change" anything, he didn't have correct "change" for my paper money! So, I pulled all of my money off to the side of the counter to get out of the way - because the people behind me were starting to get angry too - and I counted out my money coin by coin. I had just enough in coins. I stuffed the rest of my money in my pocket and got back in line.

It was even longer than the first one, but I waited patiently and finally got back to the window. The attendant looked up and was surprised to see me. Then, he started to laugh. "You!" he said. I gave him my exact change and then he waved it off and said "You don't have to pay this time. You worked hard enough. Here are your tokens." I had made a friend. If only we had had an interpreter, we wouldn't have had to go through all of that.

Have you ever read a Bible verse or heard something the Pastor says and not understood what it means? There are lots of parts of the Bible that can be confusing or that don't seem to make sense in our daily lives.

The people in this room study the Bible and try to put into practice what it means. Whenever you don't understand something you are reading in the Bible, the Sunday school teachers, the pastor, your parents all can help you interpret God's word. When you and I begin to understand more, we can be interpreters for others too.

Let us pray...

Lord, help us to hear your words in a way that we understand and surround us with interpreters, who can teach us the meaning of your word. Amen.

WHAT MAKES YOU KIND

Get Yourself Focused

When someone is unkind or mean to us, it is easy to react in a negative way, but while that may feel good in the moment, it does nothing to help us in the long run. When we behave in negative ways, it hurts us much more than it affects anyone else. Instead, choose to be your best self.

Preparation

- Read Matthew 5:38-42

The Story

Someone gave me a dirty look the other day and I thought "Eww. He looks really ugly!" Then...I thought "Hey, wait a minute. How dare he give me a dirty look! He doesn't even know me! Who does he think he is?" ...but later...I thought "When someone does mean things to other people, it makes the mean person ugly, not the person they are being mean to."

See, when *I* give someone a dirty look, it makes *my* face ugly - not theirs. Our actions and words show who *we are*, not anyone else. It might bother the person I give a dirty look to for a few minutes, but if they just go on about their day, they are likely to forget all about it. I, on the other hand, not only look ugly, but I probably feel pretty ugly on the inside too.

Life experiences shape us. The only thing we have any control over is how we act. If someone hurts us, our job is to forgive. If someone makes us mad, our job is to work it out with them. Each action we do is an experience we take with us for the rest of our lives. We should act in ways that we won't mind carrying around with us for that long. Everything we do brings us closer to becoming something. God has an idea of who He wants each of us to be. Be that person, by the actions *you* choose:

When you give a dirty look to someone - it makes *you* ugly.

When you are kind to someone else - it makes *you* kind.

When you are mean to someone else - it makes *you* mean.

When you give generously - it makes *you* generous.

When you hurt someone else - it makes *you* hurtful.

When you treat everyone with love - it makes *you* loving.

Let us pray...

Heavenly Father, you see each of us as something wonderful and full of potential. Help us to choose our actions and to react to others in a way that is pleasing to you, so we can become everything you plan for us to be. In your name we pray, Amen.

WHAT'S THE WORD?

Get Yourself Focused

There are lots of different versions of the Bible. Depending on what denomination or 'flavor' of religion you are, you may prefer to study one version or another. All of them are the Word of God. The more familiar we are with God's Word, the more clearly we will hear him in all the ways he speaks to us.

Preparation

- Bring several different Bibles. They can look and feel different on the outside. Include 2 or 3 different versions and bring a Bible on an electronic reader or a computer, if you are able.

The Story

There are lots of ways that God speaks to us: through pastors, friends, music, nature, animals, to name a few.

Have you ever heard God speak to you? [*Let the kids truly answer the question. Don't discount what they say. God speaks to even our littlest ones and sometimes, they know it.*] How did he speak? Was it like a small voice in your head, that wasn't yours? Maybe you had a dream about something? Did you ever feel like a good friend or maybe a relative, like your grandma was telling you something that God wanted you to know? Those are all important ways that God speaks to us. The most important way is through the Bible, though. We call it "The Word of God".

How many of you have received a Bible from the church? There are lots of different versions of the Bible. I brought several with me today. Usually the church gives one that is just for kids, like you. [*Show a couple of sections that are added for kids*]

Here are some more versions that I brought that are written for anyone. [*Show the other versions of the Bible that you brought. Let the kids look at them and pass them around. Talk about the differences on the outside.*]

Let's see what's inside, [*Read Psalm 23 all the way through from one version, then read Psalm 23:1-4a from a second version that is slightly different. I used the NIV and The Message.*] Some versions of the Bible are translations from ancient Greek and Hebrew texts. Others are paraphrases of what the original texts said.

Both of the Bibles I just read used different words, but had the same meaning. They were all spoken to humans, by God. Lots of books are good books and they teach the lessons that God wants us to learn, but the Bible is the only one that is spoken by God.

So, when a person talks to you and you think you might be hearing what God wants you to know, how can you be sure? Sometimes you can't, but if what you are hearing is good, it will not disagree with what the Bible says and some of it might even be the same things that are in the Bible, just spoken in slightly different words. The better you know The Word, the better you will be able to recognize God's voice in other places.

Let us pray...

God, we are so grateful that you have many ways to speak to us. Help us to understand the most important one, your Word, *The Bible*. Give us opportunities to read it and share it with our family and friends. Use it to bring us closer to you. Amen.

A DISTINCTIVE WALK

Get Yourself Focused

Each of us is unique. As children grow and refine their belief in God, they need to think about what that uniqueness means to how they will live out their faith. As they do this, they will develop their own distinctive walk.

Preparation

- Read Timothy 1:7

Story

My grade school principal had a very distinctive walk. She used to wear low heeled, sturdy pumps that made noise every time she walked down the hall. I can still hear it now, click-click, click-click, click, click-tee, click, clack. If you were doing something you shouldn't be doing, it made a chill run down your spine and you stopped whatever it was in a hurry! She was a stern woman sometimes, but fair. She loved every student in the building as if they were her own children. She showed that in lots of ways.

She remembered everyone's name and often important things like when their birthday was or what type of activity they liked to do. She always asked about you, when she was talking to you. She never talked about herself. She rewarded hard work and stuck up for kids who got pushed around. When the cheerleaders needed new uniforms and the budget was too tight to get some, she bought fabric and made them herself. They looked great too. Way better than the old ones. Her caring for children was part of what defined her distinctive walk.

Each of us is walking through life, making decisions about how we will act, and what activities we will spend time on; who we hang out with, and how we express ourselves. Other people see us making this walk and it defines us. As Christians, we don't take this walk by ourselves. We constantly seek Jesus' guidance and try to be like He was. No two people do that in the same way, though.

I have one friend who a few times a year, fasts and prays to focus his intentions on God's will for his life. Another friend of mine gets close to God through her music. I have another friend who is a tremendous cook and he uses his barbecue business to reach out to others and sponsor fundraisers. There are lots of ways to take your Christian walk.

There is no one right way, but God doesn't want us to be timid about it. 2 Timothy 1:7 says "For the spirit God gave us does not make us timid, but gives us power, love and self-discipline." Twenty years from now, what do you want people to say about you and how you lived your life? Find what you are passionate about and then make it part of your faith walk.

Let Us Pray...

Lord, we are grateful that you walk with us each day as we grow and learn. Help us to decide what will be distinctive about our walk and how we will define ourselves to others. In your name we pray. Amen.

LOOKING THROUGH THE SCREEN

Get Yourself Focused

It is so easy to get caught up in our external appearance and the outward impressions we make on our neighbors. We sometimes forget that what is important is what God thinks of us, not what people think of us. He looks through our external 'screens' and sees us on the inside. That's how we should view each other too.

Preparation

- Bring some pictures to show that have been taken through a window screen. You can have printed pictures to pass around to the children or display them on a projector screen for the whole congregation to see.

Story

Today I brought a few pictures of birds out my back window. We have feeders in our backyard and we see all sorts of beautiful birds throughout the day. When I was looking out my window, I thought I was taking "postcard perfect" pictures, but when I took a closer look at them later on, I realized you could see more of the window screen, than the birds. That's not what I wanted at all!

I've often noticed that when I look at a scene in front of me and then take a picture of it, the camera sees it differently than I remember seeing it. The camera picks up every little detail, even the ugly or unimportant things, that my eye ignores. Cameras don't sort out what's important and what's not, when they look at something. They just take it all in and give equal significance to everything they see. Our brains look at a scene and choose what matters and what does not and creates a mental picture from those parts.

My view through my screened window reminded me of God's vision. We were made in God's image and I think our eyes see things much the same way He does. When He looks out His window at us, He sees our intentions, our spirit, the essence of us. He doesn't notice our clothes or our hair style or the leftover breakfast on our mouth. He sees the beautiful person that we are and He loves it!

I have a challenge for you this week. I want you to try to look at the people around you the way God does. Don't notice what they look like or how they act, try to see who they are. It may take some practice, before you get the hang of it, but once you do it a few times, it will be easy to do all the time. Next Sunday, I will ask you how it went!

Let Us Pray...

God, we know that what is on our outside is not nearly as important as what is on our inside. Sometimes we forget that what is on other people's inside is more important than their outside too. Help us to see people as you do. In Jesus name we pray, Amen.

GOD'S TOOLBOX

Get Yourself Focused

Whenever you want to accomplish a project, you need the right tools. We are God's custom made tools. He uses us for different types of projects, each in different ways. We should never worry that we are doing something differently from someone else or that we don't fit a particular job. We are each specially made to do the work of God.

Preparation

- Bring a toolbox with various types of tools (except a hammer)

- Also, bring two boards to nail together

- Arrange for a member of the congregation to have the hammer and bring it up to you, when you ask

- Read 1 Corinthians 12:4-11

The Story

I'm going to demonstrate something for you this morning. I brought along these two boards and a couple of nails. I want you to watch, while I nail these boards together and then we are going to talk about how God uses tools.

[*Get the boards and nails ready to be nailed and then look in your toolbox for something to nail them with.*] Here, this is a really nice screwdriver. I think it will do the trick. [*Try to screw the nails in or pry a hole in the wood for the nail, with the end.*] Hmm. That's going to take too long, what else is in here? [*Try to nail the boards with a saw, a wrench, etc. End up by just banging one of the tools on the nail to try to get it to go in. The children may start trying to help you or give you advice. Talk with them about what is happening.]*

You know what would work really well, is a hammer. [*Turn to the congregation.*] Does anyone have a hammer? Oh, thank you, so much! [*Hammer in the nail.*] You can't use one tool for every job. Tools need to be made for a particular use and some of them can do several things, but none of them can do everything.

Now...what did all of this have to do with how God uses tools? We are God's custom made tools. [*Read 1 Corinthians 12:4-11*] Each of us is good at some things and not others. God uses us to do His work in many different ways. Just like we use these tools. We should never worry, if we aren't good at something or if we do things differently than other people. God made each of us for a special purpose that no one else can do and He will use us, if we let Him, to do His work.

Let us pray...

Dear God, show me where you want me to be useful. Help me develop the talents You have given me to do the work of your kingdom. In your precious and loving name, Amen.

PULLING DANDELIONS

Get Yourself Focused

We are all familiar with weeds in our lawns and gardens. They make a great analogy for the type of behavior that we don't want to show toward our neighbors.

Preparation

- Read Matthew 7:12

The Story

I was pulling dandelions in my garden the other day and thinking about how difficult they are to get rid of. Then I thought to myself, why do I want to get rid of them? They are actually pretty to look at, especially when there is a whole field of them. Even when they are dying, their fluffy white puff balls look pretty, until they let go of each of their seeds and let the wind carry it to start a new plant. Dandelions are healthy too. They make a tasty addition to salad or soup. So why do we think dandelions are weeds?

What is a weed anyway? [T*ake a few answers from the kids*] My dictionary says that a weed is a plant that is not valued where it is growing and one that tends to overgrow or choke out more desirable plants.

Weeds often grow and take over from other plants, because they adapt to change well. Weeds are usually some of the first plants to start coming up after the snow melts and they have lots of seeds that are easy to spread, just like dandelions do. Those aren't bad things. As a matter of fact, they are good things. The problem with weeds, is that anywhere they show up, they take over and make it difficult, if not impossible for other plants to grow. They don't want to live *with* other plants. They want to live *instead* of them. We should take care of the our own gardens, so they grow good plants, instead of the weeds.

People can sometimes be like dandelions. Most of the time it's not on purpose. If people are worried that there won't be enough of something they want or need, sometimes they hoard it or try to keep other people from having it. If someone doesn't know that the way they get food or throw away trash or consume water affects other people, they might choose the wrong way to do those things. The Bible tells us we should love our neighbors as ourselves and treat them as we would want to be treated. [*Matthew 7:12*]

Let us pray...

Lord help us to know how to care for your earth and our fellow neighbors in it. We want to please you in everything we do. In your name we pray, Amen.

...THAT'S WHAT LITTLE BELLS ARE MADE OF

Get Yourself Focused

Today's lesson does not have a specific Bible verse to refer to, but it is based on several lessons taught in the New Testament. Surround yourself with people, things and practices that are part of God's teaching and you will be able to make beautiful music, like a bell.

Preparation

- Bring several different kinds of bells made from different materials, you can even include things like sleigh bells or wind chimes. If you don't have a variety of bells, you could do the same lesson with household items such as pots & pans, pan lids, a hollow piece of wood, a plastic bowl, a glass dish, etc.

Story

I brought several different bells with me today. I thought it would be interesting to hear what they sound like. [*Have some volunteers take turns tapping on or ringing the different items.*] Some of the bells sound tinny, others sound flat. Some have a beautiful ring tone. Depending on what they are made of, they make a different sound. For example, this one is just thin aluminum. It sounds kind of clanky, doesn't it? This one is made of brass and has a clear, musical tone. This one is a silver sleigh bell. It has a rich sound when it rings.

Each of these bells are unique. Which one did you like best? Which one wasn't very nice to listen to? Several of these bells sounded nice, but they were different.

We are kind of like these bells. We are all made different and we all have our own "sound". What we are "made of" is determined by the things we put into our lives - the people we hang out with, the activities we choose, the way we treat other people and ourselves. Rules like "don't do drugs" or "do unto others as you would have them do unto you" or "look both ways before you cross the street" are telling you to not be "made of" unclean, hurtful, cruel things and to choose healthy, thoughtful, safe things to be in your life. When we put only the best things in our lives, we become people who "ring" more clearly and who make sounds that others are drawn to.

Let Us Pray…

Lord, help us to make our lives pleasant sounds for You to hear. We want the things we do and the people we become, to be representations of Your good work. In your name we pray, Amen.

HOW YOU CUT THE DECK

Get Yourself Focused

The minor prophets make up the last part of the Old Testament, as we know it. Some of their text describes sad, difficult times. But that's not the end of the story! The New Testament not only made the Bible bigger, it changed the perspective of the story. The Good News of Jesus Christ changed everything.

Preparation

- Become familiar with the minor prophets at the end of the Old Testament, particularly Malachi 4:5-6
- Bring a deck of cards

Story

> I have a deck of cards with me this morning. I need some help cutting them. [*Show them how you shuffle, then cut the deck, with one of the kids' help.*] When you cut the deck, the card that was on the bottom, ends up in the middle of the deck. See? Sometimes, what seems like the bottom of the pile - or the end of something, is actually just the middle of something...or maybe the moment before something completely new is about to happen.
>
> At the end of the Old Testament, there are several books called "The Minor Prophets", they are Hosea, Joel, Amos, Obadiah, Jonah, Micah, Nahum, Habakkuk, Zephaniah, Haggai, Zechariah and Malachi. Before the New Testament was written, Malachi was the end of the Bible. Now, it's in the middle of the Bible, right before the New Testament.

The Minor Prophets talk about times when things weren't going so well for the people of Israel. They talk about God being jealous and His people turning away from Him or getting caught up in things they shouldn't be doing. Each of these prophets shares what God has said concerning disobedience to His laws and consequences for not following God. Here is the last part of Malachi, the last book in the Old Testament [*Read Malachi 4:5-6*]. That sounds pretty awful, doesn't it?

…but then I turn the page in my Bible and it says "The New Testament of our Lord and Savior Jesus Christ". The Good News! The New Testament begins with the lineage of Jesus and the story of His birth.

When Jesus came, everything at the bottom of the deck, became somewhere in the middle and the introduction of something wonderful and new. Aren't we blessed to be living after Jesus was born?

Let Us Pray…

Lord, thank you for the whole story of the Bible. The Good News of Jesus' birth gives us the right perspective to read the rest of Your Word and gives us hope for the future. You are so good to us! In your name we pray, Amen.

TWIST TIES DON'T LAST FOREVER

Get Yourself Focused

We all have potential and God given talents. We should recognize how wonderful that is and how important it is to use them starting TODAY, because life on this earth doesn't go on forever.

Preparation

- Read Matthew 25:23, 1 Peter 4:10-11

- Bring a twist tie

Story

I have a habit of saving little odds and ends that might be useful someday…rubber bands, blank envelopes, twist ties, paper bags, shipping boxes….I learned this habit from my grandfather, who grew up during the depression and had a talent for making something out of nothing.

My son has grown up with this habit of mine and knows that before he throws something away, he should check if it has a future potential use. So, the other day, he saw me throw away a twist tie. *Right away, he said, "Mommy, you just threw away a twist tie!"* "I know," I said. "But that's a waste of a twist tie," he pointed out. "Well, that twist tie was worn out. It was time to throw it away. Twist ties don't last forever, you know." I answered back.

Then it struck me - twist ties do not last forever. Nothing does. Someday, the little pieces of magnet and partially used erasers, scrap pieces of paper, snippets of thread and twist ties, that have been carefully tucked away in various places of my house, will disintegrate into dust. Just like the drawer they are kept in and the cabinet that houses that drawer. The floor that the cabinet sits on and the walls that hold up the roof over the floor. All of that will turn to recycled lumber or wood shavings or just plain old, ordinary dust. Someday.

Today, it has potential. A twist tie could be used to hold a bag of homemade bread closed or to attach a bow to a wreath. The plastic coating could be taken off of it and it could be used as wire to make a homemade battery. It could be all sorts of things, if it were given a chance. What a shame to throw away twist ties that still have potential. And what a shame to hang on to twist ties that need to go.

Each of us has God given talents and lots of potential. We also have a great big gift called "life". God gave us that gift, so we could make the most of ourselves and contribute to this wonderful world that He made. At your young age, you should be exploring. Try new things, find out what interests you. If you find something you really love to do, get good at it, so you can do it more. Practice the activities that inspire you. Learn as much as you can about areas that excite you. Discover who you are and what you are made of.

God had a plan, when He made you. He brought you into this world at this particular time and place to do something special. Something that can only be done by you, the way you do things. Go find out what that is! All of us will be done with this life someday and we want God to say "Well done, good and faithful servant." [*Matthew 25:23*]

Let Us Pray...

To close today, I am going to read a Bible verse to you. [*Read 1 Peter 4:10-11*]

HOLY JEANS

Get Yourself Focused

How we treat ourselves and other people is important, because as children of God, we are the place where the Holy Spirit dwells. It is important that we behave and think like the Holy people that God made us to be.

Preparation

- Read Genesis 1:26, Galatians 3:23-29
- Wear a pair of jeans with holes in them or have one of the kids wear a pair to church

Story

My son's favorite pair of jeans are the ones he has on today. They fit him well and they are comfortable and stretched out. They also have two big holes in them - one in each knee. Do any of you have a pair of jeans like that? He calls them his 'hole-y jeans', so he convinced me that I should let him wear them to church. What better place to wear something that's 'holy'?

Actually, we all have holy genes. I don't mean 'blue jeans' I mean 'genes', as in the traits that are passed down from one generation to the next. Like blue eyes or black hair, crooked teeth or lots of freckles. Several places in the Bible tell us that we are God's children. We were made in His image - Holy in His eyes. [*Read Genesis 1:26 & Galatians 3:23-29*]

So if each of us are Holy, then it matters how we treat ourselves and each other, doesn't it? We should treat ourselves with respect and treat our neighbors as ourselves. We should behave like children of someone important. That means we are thoughtful of others and confident in the abilities God has given us. We need to speak the truth and not lie. We should look for the best in each situation and try when we can to create good, where we are.

We talk a lot about how what is on our inside is more important than what is on the outside and how our spirits are more important than our bodies, but we should take care of our bodies too. We shouldn't eat things that are bad for us or take drugs. We should get plenty of exercise and a good amount of sleep. All of these things are smart things for anyone who wants to be healthy to do. Being healthy is important, but as Christians, it's more than just that. We honor God by taking care of ourselves. The Holy Spirit dwells within us and so our body is its home. By taking care of ourselves, we honor our 'holy genes'.

Let Us Pray…

God thank you for the gift of our favorite holy genes. Help us feel comfortable with them and to honor you, by taking good care of them with our words, our actions and our thoughts. In your name we pray. Amen.

TRUE REFLECTIONS

Get Yourself Focused

As children grow and become more aware of who they are and who they want to become, it is important for them to find positive influences in their lives. It may be difficult to see at first, but with the right 'reflections' they will have a better understanding of themselves.

Preparation

- Bring a mirror with you

The Story

I brought a mirror with me today. They are fascinating things and truthful. A mirror only ever looks like what is in front of it. It can't ever look like anything else. So, if something ugly is in front of it, it looks ugly. If something scary is in front of it, it looks scary. If something beautiful is in front of it…well, you get the idea.

Sometimes, when I look in a mirror, I see things in new ways. For example, have you ever looked at yourself in the mirror, while you are brushing your teeth or getting dressed? Have you ever thought "Hey, I look GOOD!" Mirrors allow us to see ourselves from the outside. There is no other way to do that. A change in perspective can be good.

When things are not going well for us, it is easy to focus on the negative things around us or the negative things about ourselves. We get frustrated and wish we were different or wish the things around us were different. That is the perfect time for a mirror. And I don't just mean one like I brought today. I mean a person, who can be like a mirror. Someone who knows us well and knows all the good things about us. Someone who can remind us of who we really are and who we can become.

It might be a good friend, who tells us what they like about us. Maybe it's a teacher who encourages us to try something that we hadn't considered doing, because they see we have a natural talent for it. Maybe our mirror is someone who doesn't particularly like us and gives us a hard time at school. They might draw out confidence to stand up for ourselves. Sometimes the people who seem the most unlovable are the one most in need of love. Perhaps they need a mirror, themselves.

How could you be a mirror for someone else? How can you reflect positive things back to another person you care about? You could be a good listener. Be present for other people, go to their activities. Tell them great things about what they are doing. Be open and caring to people around you - not just those who make you feel good, but those who need you to make them feel good too.

Sometimes, the easiest way to create more light, more openness, more goodness, is to reflect it. Find the people in your life who can be a mirror for you, when you need one. And whenever you have the chance, be a mirror, yourself. Focus on the positive. If you see something worthwhile happening, cheer it on or better yet, participate in it.

Let us pray...

Lord, thank you for the truthful mirrors in our lives who reflect our own positive qualities back to us and see ourselves as we truly are. Help us to learn how to be those kind of mirrors for others, as well. In your loving name we pray, Amen.

BREAD OR COOKIES? - YES!

Get Yourself Focused

Lots of times, things don't seem even or fair in life. God has the big picture, though, and He always gives us what we need. More than that, God is benevolent. He often gives us what we want too.

Preparation

- Read Matthew 7:9-11
- Bring cookies or homemade bread (or both!) for the kids

Story

My nephew went to a summer camp a couple of years ago, where they learned all sorts of awesome things. They learned how to take care of sheep and goats & chickens. They made shadow art and kaleidoscopes. They swam and collected bugs. On Monday, when I picked him up, my nephew had a fresh piece of homemade bread for me. It was wonderful!

I thanked him and asked him to tell me all about it. He said making bread was fun, but he was a little upset. "They divided us into groups and my group made bread, but Evan's group got to make cookies! It's not fair." I told him I thought the homemade bread was just as yummy as the cookies. He disagreed.

Everyday, when I came to pick him up, he would tell me what he learned and share what he made and there were a lot of yummy things he would share with me…but not cookies. He was so disappointed. No matter how much I encouraged him and reminded him of all the good things he did get - all he could think about was how he didn't get to make cookies.

Then, Friday afternoon, when I picked him up, he jumped into the car and handed me a cookie. Look what I got! We made cookies today and Evan's group made bread!" "And what was it you were so worried about?" I asked him. "Nothing, I guess," he grinned.

Sometimes it may feel like everyone around us has a better life than we do or gets their way more than we do. It's not true. God loves each of us the same and doesn't play favorites. God knows what we need and He gives it to us even when we don't ask for it. But He also knows what we want and what will make us happy. If it is something that won't harm us or anyone else, He is more than glad to give it to us. God doesn't make us choose bread or cookies - He gives us both! Sometimes, you just have to be patient.

Let Us Pray…

God you are so generous with us. You give us everything we need and more, just because you love us. Help us to trust that you know what is best and to be grateful for all of Your gifts. Amen.

JOSEPH GLOWS IN THE DARK

Get Yourself Focused

Today's story focuses on Joseph of Arimathea, the man who buried Jesus. Joseph is the first believer in Luke to act on Jesus' example, after His death. Despite a bleak situation, Joseph sees something he can do to make it better. His actions are the first glow of light, even before Jesus rises from the dead.

Preparation

- Read Luke 23:44-56

- Bring examples of lights that do not require electricity to work. Also bring glow sticks to pass out to the children at the end.

The Story

How many of you know the story of Good Friday, the day that Jesus died on the cross? Let me read a description of it to you from my Bible. [*Read Luke 23:44-49*] Just imagine you were a follower or family member of Jesus on that day. It would probably be the most horrible day you've ever had. How sad and dark.

In the next part of the story, though, there is a man that often gets left out when we talk about what happened on Good Friday. His name was Joseph and he knew how to glow in the dark!

Joseph had been a member of the council that decided Jesus should be killed, but he didn't agree with them. After Jesus died, he took Jesus' body and arranged for a tomb and buried Him. It was a comforting thing to do for the women who loved Jesus. And when everyone else around had shocked and sad reactions, Joseph took action to do a good thing in a very dark time. Jesus hadn't even risen yet, but there was already a glow of light.

Some types of light use fire to burn brightly, like this candle, but it require matches or a lighter to get it going. Some lights are like this flashlight and need batteries to light up. When the batteries die, the light goes out. Other types of light use electricity, like the lights that light up our sanctuary today. If there was a thunderstorm and the electricity went out, they wouldn't work. Good Friday was kind of like a thunderstorm. The disciples felt hopeless and disconnected from the light of Jesus. The whole sky was dark and the world seemed black.

The type of light that Joseph had on Good Friday doesn't need to be plugged in or lit by fire to glow. He teaches us that in times of greatest darkness, we need to look inside ourselves, where we keep the love from friends and family; our sweetest memories, and God's gift of the Holy Spirit. That's where light that glows in the dark can be found.

I brought glow sticks for each of you today, to remind you of the kind of light that glows from inside, no matter how dark it is. Let's wear them today, so that everyone in the congregation will think of the light inside when they look at us!

Let us pray...

Lord Jesus, thank you for the lessons of Good Friday and the light that you have put inside of each of us. In your loving name we pray. Amen.

WE ARE WAITING

Get Yourself Focused

Christmas is an exciting time for everyone, not just children. The season of Advent is important in our anticipation of Christmas, because it teaches us to not only wait for the holiday of Christmas, but to prepare our hearts for the coming of Jesus, as well.

Preparation

- Read Titus 2:11-13

The Story

So, who can tell me how many days are left until Christmas? It's not far away, is it? I can hardly WAIT until it gets here! How about you?

Do you like waiting? Me either. Well, there are some things I could wait for, like having to get a filling at the dentist or having to do chores when I get home. ...oh yes, I have chores too. That's not just a kid thing. Some things I can wait for. But, Christmas? That is hard to wait for.

What do you do at your house to get ready for Christmas? Do you shop for gifts for friends and family? Does someone in your house make cookies or special food? Do you put up a tree or lights? As we are preparing for the actual day of Christmas, we can also be preparing our hearts to let Jesus in.

Did you know that the church has a season of waiting? It's called "Advent". It begins 4 Sundays before Christmas (that's today) and it ends on Christmas Day. I think it's great that we made a whole season of waiting. Well, we're doing it anyway. We might as well have specific things we do to remind us why we are waiting and to get ready for what is to come. Right?

Do you see the wreath with the candles up on the altar? That is our advent wreath. It is one of the things we do during Advent, to prepare for Jesus. Each Sunday we light a new candle to represent something for us to focus on during that week and then on Christmas, we light the last one. The four candles around the wreath represent the virtues we are given as Christians: Hope, Joy, Peace and Love.

The first week we are going to focus on "Hope". We have Hope, because not only did Jesus come to earth once a long time ago, but He is coming again. We don't know exactly when...so we are waiting.

This week, think about how you might be Hope to other people, who are feeling hopeless right now. Maybe you can donate your time to a food pantry or to help a neighbor carry heavy packages inside. You could show kindness to people at school - not just the ones you know well, but the ones you haven't met yet also. Set aside some money to donate to a good organization like Heifer Project or New Community Project or The Salvation Army. Can you think of any others? I'll bet if you talked it over with your parents this afternoon, you could come up with some other ways you might be Hope this season while we wait for Christmas.

Let Us Pray…

Dear Father in Heaven, thank you for the gift of Jesus and the Hope we have, because of Him. Help us to prepare not only our houses and our yards for Christmas this year, but also our hearts to receive Jesus too. Help us do kind and loving things for our neighbors, while we wait, so people will know what Hope is through us. In your name we pray, Amen.

NO NEED TO WAIT - LOVE IS HERE!

Get Yourself Focused

This Advent lesson can be used any time of year to talk about the love of Christ and how it lives in us.

Preparation

- Read 1 Corinthians 13:4-7 and Matthew 25:44-46

- If you are able to, play Matthew West's song "Do Something" at the end of your story. It is a wonderful testament to our call to be the body of Christ in the world.

The Story

We talk about "Love" a lot. There are "Love Songs" on the radio. We have Valentine's Day to express love to one another. We talk about different kinds of love – for your mom and dad; for a husband or wife; for your friends, for your pets, for your favorite type of ice cream (there's a special type of love for that!). ...but what is "Love"?

One of the best known passages in the Bible is 1 Corinthians 13. I'm going to read you part of it [*Read 1 Corinthians 13:4-7*]. That is the best definition of "Love" that we have. You and I are at church right now and it's full of people who know the Bible well. Many of us are memorizing verses from the Bible, ourselves. We can read passages like this to know what love is. But what if we were someone who didn't go to church very often – or not at all, maybe? What if we had never read the Bible? How would we know what love was then? [*Let them share some answers. Children often have great, surprising ideas about things like this.*]

What if we were an example of love? What if someone who doesn't hear the Bible very often saw us being kind or patient? What if they saw us not being jealous when someone else got something better than us or not bragging about what we can do really well. Would that give them an idea what love is? We are the body of Christ. We are called by Jesus to share God's love with everyone we come in contact with. Sometimes, that just means being like Christ.

I'm going to play a song for you by Matthew West. It's called "Do Something", from his album *Into the Light*. Listen to the words carefully. The song is partly based on Matthew 25:44-46, where Jesus tells his disciples that when they help others, they are helping Jesus Christ, Himself.

Let us pray...

Jesus, as we wait for Christmas and the coming of You, show us how to be "Love" in the world. We want to use you as the example of how to treat other people, give of ourselves and spread your love throughout the world. In your heavenly name we pray. Amen.

[1] *Written by Matthew West • Copyright © Sony/ATV Music Publishing LLC, Warner/Chappell Music, Inc.*

THE JOY OF THE WISE MEN

Get Yourself Focused

We often think of joy as being a *lot* of happiness. It is much more than that and it can be felt, even when you are not happy. This story can be used during Advent, but it can also be adapted to other times of the year to demonstrate joy.

Preparation

- Read Matthew 2:9-10

The Story

We are one week closer to Christmas. Are you excited? Me too! There are lots of things about Christmas to look forward to. Spending time with family. Enjoying good food. Sharing gifts with one another. Seeing friends we don't get to see very often. There are lots of things to celebrate! Those things make me happy – very, very happy. But, there's something that gives me a more lasting, deep down feeling and it's the whole reason we have Christmas in the first place. It's the coming of Jesus Christ and that give me joy.

Joy is more than just being extra-happy. Joy is a deep down good feeling that never goes away, even when we are sad. It's a feeling that says "Today is a horrible day, but I know God loves me and He will not leave my side, no matter what." It can also say "Today is my birthday and I am having the best time! Thank you God for all of the good things you give me!" Joy tells us that no matter what is going on here on earth, there is a bigger picture that God is watching over and He always makes things right.

In the Bible, it talks about three people who felt great joy at the coming of Jesus – the Wise Men. They journeyed from a long way away. They were told to follow a particular star in the East and it would take them to where the Savior was. They were told he would be a great king and they brought Him gifts that you would give a king. They had some adventures along the way, but they made it safely by doing what God told them and keeping their eyes on that star. [Read Matthew 2:9-10] Imagine how they felt, when they finally arrived where the star led them, they were not just happy. They were joyous! They must have tried to picture how Jesus was going to change everything and make the whole world a different place, from then on. It wasn't as if they had just been served their favorite dessert – they were meeting the baby who would become the Savior!

Joy lifts us up. No matter where we start, joy will take us higher. Sharing our joy can do that for others too. During this week of Advent, whatever we are doing, let's practice doing it with joy. If things are going your way, express joy. If you are having a rotten day, remember how much God loves you anyway and express joy. If you see someone else having a rotten day, lift them up and forget about your own worries. Share your joy. Christmas is almost here, so grab some Joy and pass it around!

Let us pray...

Lord, Christmastime is an easy time to start focusing on joy. There is so much around us. Help us to feel it deep down in our hearts, so that when this season is over we take it with us into the year to come. Amen.

PEACE LIKE A RIVER

Get Yourself Focused

In our busy, world that is always striving and achieving, it is difficult to visualize what peace actually is. A river is a great example of what it truly feels and looks like.

Preparation

- Read John 7:37-38

- In this story, we talk about the song I've Got Peace Like a River. At the beginning of the story, I encourage you to sing at least a little part of the song, so the kids will recognize what you are talking about. At the end if you have time, sing the whole song and invite the congregation to join you. If you aren't able to sing the song, just close with the prayer.

The Story

Lately, I have been thinking about what peace means during Advent. There is a song that has been running through my head. How many of you have ever heard the song, *Peace Like a River*? It talks about having Peace like a river, Love like an ocean and Joy like a fountain. [*Sing the first part, so they can hear the tune.*]

A river actually is a very good way to describe what peace is like. That's probably why the person who wrote that song chose a river to compare peace to.

What is a river like? Does a river sit still? No. It flows, doesn't it? What does the water look like when it flows down a river? Sometimes it rushes really fast; sometimes it trickles slowly. It depends on how much water there is in the river and whether it flows down a big hill or not. It's always moving though.

Is it straight? Most of the time it's kind of winding, isn't it? Some rivers like the Mississippi or the Nile River are long or deep. Other rivers, like the one near us [*Fill in a local smaller river.*] are more shallow and you can see the bottom in spots.

What is the bottom of a river like? Sometimes it has mud and rocks or fallen trees and sticks. It's not very smooth, is it? As the water flows over all of the things on the bottom and sides of the riverbed, it may trip a little, but it keeps going. Sounds kind of like our own lives, doesn't it?

Rivers are connected. They take water from one place to another. No matter what shape or size a river is, it's always connected at one end for water to flow in and one end, where water flows out.

The peace of Jesus Christ flows on and when we are connected to Him, it flows through us. We don't ever have to worry about anything, because God will take care of us and get us over the rocks and sticks. He will guide our paths, even when they aren't perfectly straight. All we need to do is flow along, never stopping, and stay connected. That's peace, just like a river.

[*If you have time, sing "Peace Like a River".*]

Let us pray...

God grant us peace. As we look forward to Christmas, help us understand how to have the peace that Jesus spoke about in our own lives and flowing through us, just like a river. In your name we pray, Amen.

ABOUT THE AUTHOR

Kate Finney writes from her home in Northern Indiana, where she lives with her husband and son. This is her second book of children's worship stories and a compliment to the website worshipwithkids.com where she shares more stories and worship ideas twice a month. You can contact Kate directly from her website or e-mail her at kate@worshipwithkids.com.

www.ingramcontent.com/pod-product-compliance
Lightning Source LLC
Chambersburg PA
CBHW061248040426
42444CB00010B/2293